Date: 12/21/18

J 591.5 WHO
Whoa, that's strange!

Introduction

Nature is filled with some amazing creatures. From ocean bottoms to mountain tops, from hot deserts to freezing tundra, the *Ugh! Yuck! and Whoa!* books highlight the most extreme animals: the grossest, the deadliest, the strangest, and the ugliest! This book is all about animals with strange behaviors and skills. Species of animals have evolved to have certain skills, habits, or body parts. To evolve means to change over time. These skills and behaviors are adaptations. An adaptation is something an animal or other living has or does that helps it survive and reproduce (make more living things like itself) in its environment. Humans can't breathe water or live in the extreme cold. But other animals can live in those conditions! Read on to learn about some of the strangest animal adaptations that nature has to offer. This Strange Scale meter will show how unusual each animal can be!

STRANGE SCALE

MEDIUM

WOODPECKER

Ugh! Yuck! and Whoa!

Whoa, That's Strange!

WORLD
BOOK

World Book, Inc.
180 North LaSalle Street
Suite 900
Chicago, Illinois 60601
USA

For information about other World Book publications, visit our website at **www.worldbook.com** or call **1-800-WORLDBK (967-5325)**.

Library of Congress Cataloging-in-Publication data has been applied for.
Title: Ugh! Yuck! and Whoa! Whoa, That's Strange!
ISBN: 978-0-7166-3715-8

Ugh! Yuck! and Whoa!
ISBN: 978-0-7166-3708-0 (set, hc)

Also available as:
ISBN: 978-0-7166-3723-3 (e-book)

Printed in China by Shenzhen Wing King Tong Paper Products Co, Ltd., Shenzhen, Guangdong
1st printing July 2018

STAFF

Executive Committee

President
Jim O'Rourke

Vice President and Editor in Chief
Paul A. Kobasa

Vice President, Finance
Donald D. Keller

Vice President, Marketing
Jean Lin

Vice President, International
Maksim Rutenberg

Vice President, Technology
Jason Dole

Director, Human Resources
Bev Ecker

Editorial

Director, Print Publishing
Tom Evans

Writer
Grace Guibert

Editor
Will Adams

Manager, Contracts & Compliance (Rights & Permissions)
Loranne K. Shields

Manager, Indexing Services
David Pofelski

Librarian
S. Thomas Richardson

Digital

Director, Digital Product Development
Erika Meller

Digital Product Manager
Jonathan Wills

Manufacturing/ Production

Manufacturing Manager
Anne Fritzinger

Proofreader
Nathalie Strassheim

Graphics and Design

Senior Art Director
Tom Evans

Senior Designer
Don Di Sante

Media Editor
Rosalia Bledsoe

Special thanks to:

Nature Picture Library

Woodpeckers use their beaks to poke holes into trees. Then, they use their tongues to grab their food! Woodpecker tongues are extremely long and sticky with a sharp tip.

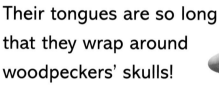

Their tongues are so long that they wrap around woodpeckers' skulls!

Whoa!

MUDSKIPPER

Mudskippers are a type of fish that can live out of the water! Most fish need to stay in the water to breathe. But mudskippers can live on land for hours and even days. They are called mudskippers because of the way they move on land. Mudskippers push themselves with their fins, and it looks like they are skipping!

SNOW MONKEY

The snow monkey, also called the Japanese macaque *(muh KAK)*, lives farther north than any other kind of monkey. It has a thick coat of fur to keep it warm during Japan's cold winters. But it also relaxes in warm volcanic springs. The springs are like hot tubs for monkeys!

Cold-Weather Creatures

Lots of animals live in cold places. They have adapted to live where it's freezing outside! Warm fur, other special body parts, and light colors of hair or feathers are some things that help animals survive in the cold and snow.

Yakutian horse

Penguin

Ptarmigan

Walrus

Dall sheep

Polar bear

HAMERKOP

This bird has some strange behaviors. They look like funny dances! Hamerkops will run around each other in circles. They flap their wings and raise their chests. Sometimes, they even stand on each other's backs like gymnasts!

Ugh!

Hamerkops are hunters! They eat small animals from in and around the water, like this frog.

13

BASILISK LIZARD

These lizards can walk on water! Basilisk lizards run across water on their back legs to get away from danger. They move quickly, skipping across the water's surface. They are also strong swimmers. When their run across the water ends, basilisk lizards can dive and swim below the surface.

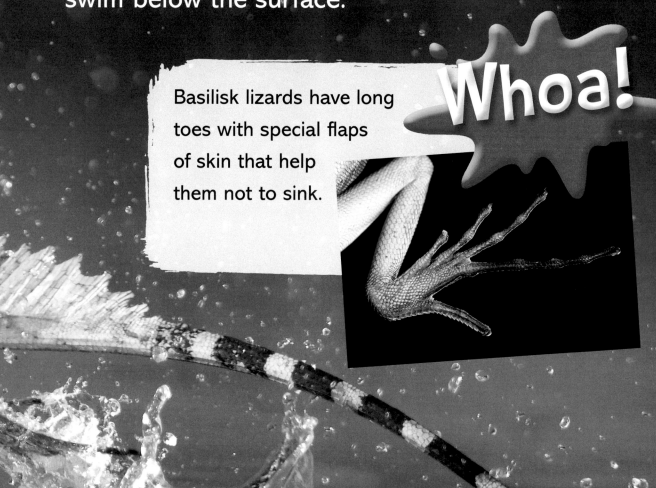

Basilisk lizards have long toes with special flaps of skin that help them not to sink.

Whoa!

NEW ZEALAND GLOWWORM

This glowing bug is a type of **fungus** gnat, an insect that feeds on **fungi** (things like yeasts, molds, and mushrooms). This **fungus** gnat lives in the wet and hot Waitomo Caves of northern New Zealand. Both young and adult glowworms give off a glowing blue light!

Whoa!

From far away, these glowworms look like strings of lights. Here's a **larva** up close!

Animals that Glow

Click beetle

Bioluminescent *(BY oh LOO muh NEHS uhnt)* animals are ones that glow! Here are some animals with the special skill to give off light.

Glowworm

Jellyfish

Squid

Lanternfish

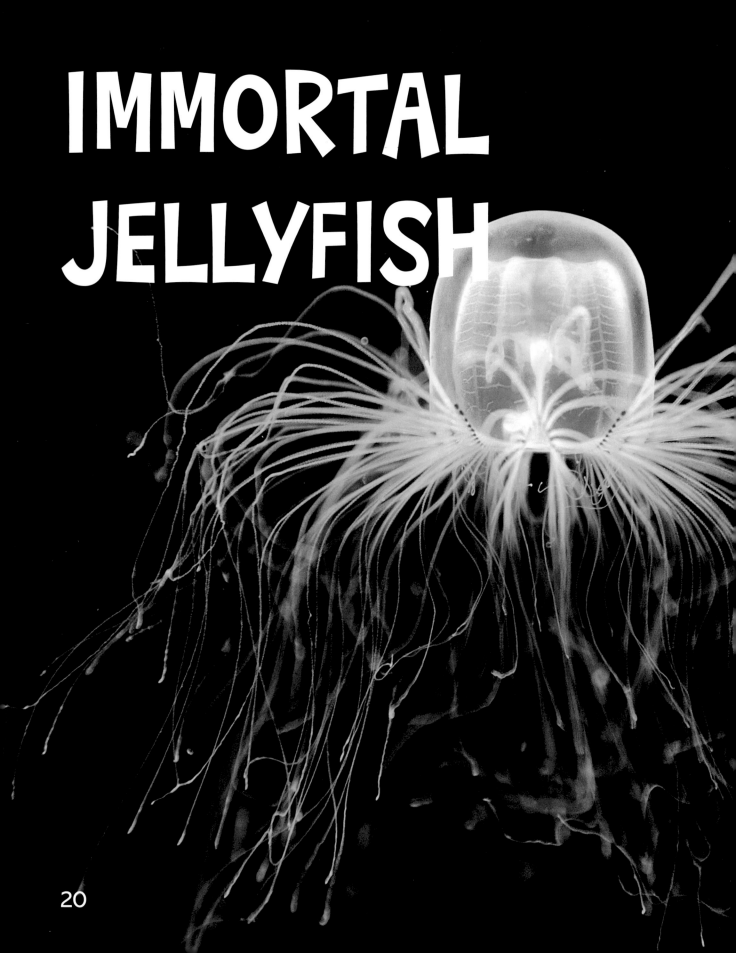

IMMORTAL JELLYFISH

To be *immortal* means to live forever. The so-called immortal jellyfish can be harmed or killed by predators, so it is not truly immortal. But it does have a strange skill! It can go back to its *polyp* form (a young growth stage). Then, it grows up all over again!

HOODED
SEAL

A male hooded seal has a funny way of attracting mates. He has a pouch inside his nose that he can inflate to form a bright red "balloon"! The hooded seal shakes his head to flap the bubbly balloon around.

STRANGE SCALE
MEDIUM

ARCHERF!SH

Archerfish are named after archers, people who shoot bows and arrows. An archerfish has its own weapon. It shoots water from its mouth like an arrow! An archerfish uses its weapon to catch its food. Archerfish can hit insects and spiders up to 3 feet (1 meter) away and knock them into the water!

Crazy Kinds of Crabs

There are hundreds of species (types) of crabs. Some of them behave in really strange ways!

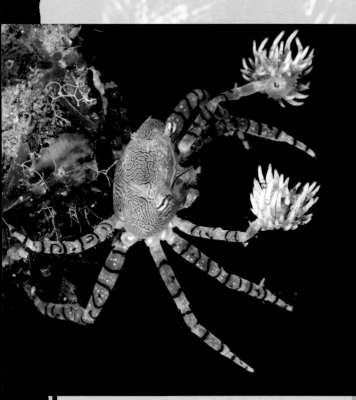

Decorator crab

Decorator crabs camouflage themselves using bits of seaweed and other living things. This helps keep them safe from predators!

Boxer crab

Sometimes called pompom crabs or cheerleader crabs, boxer crabs defend themselves with two small sea anemones *(uh NEHM uh neez)* that look a bit like pompoms!

Coconut crab

The coconut crab is the biggest crab that lives on land. It can climb up into trees to snatch coconuts! It is sometimes called the robber crab because it often steals things from people.

DIVING BELL SPIDER

Spiders live all over the world: in deserts, in cold places, high up in trees, and in our houses. The diving bell spider spends almost its whole life underwater! Like other spiders, the diving bell spider needs to breathe air. So it brings air bubbles underwater with it.

Whoa!

Scuba divers bring air underwater with them like these spiders do. Scuba divers use tanks of air to breathe from. Divers can stay below the surface for hours!

Tank of air

Scuba diver

FLAMINGO

Flamingos are pretty pink birds with long legs. They aren't always pink, though. They are born with gray feathers. They turn pink because they eat food with a natural pink coloring. You know what they say: you are what you eat!

THORNY DEVIL LIZARD

The thorny devil lizard is covered in sharp spines to protect it from attackers. It also has a *false* (fake) head behind its real head! When it feels unsafe, the thorny devil lizard protects its real head by hiding it between its front legs. It shows its false head—a large, thorny lump—instead.

SPOTTED HYENA

The spotted hyena is famous for its weird howl. It sounds like a human laughing! Other hyenas usually *scavenge,* or eat animals that are already dead, but spotted hyenas are deadly hunters. They often let out their laugh—a high "hee-hee-hee!" sound—while they are hunting.

PYGMY SHARK

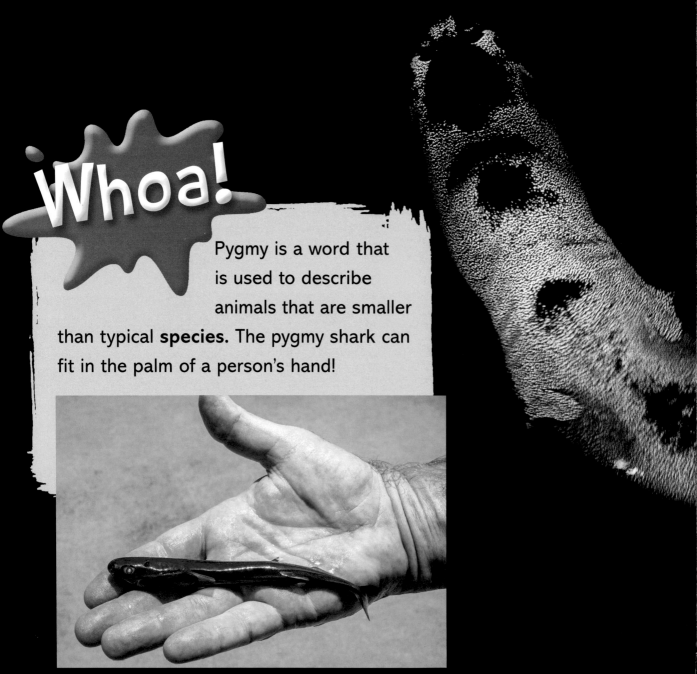

Whoa!

Pygmy is a word that is used to describe animals that are smaller than typical **species.** The pygmy shark can fit in the palm of a person's hand!

The pygmy shark is one of the smallest **species** (types) of shark. This small shark has a special skill: it glows! It might sound strange, but its glow helps it to stay hidden. The pygmy shark's belly glows. This glow blends in with the sunlight above, camouflaging the shark from predators swimming below it.

STRANGE SCALE
MEDIUM

SHORT-EARED OWL

This little owl has a big trick. The short-eared owl can turn its head upside down! Owls have very good eyesight. But they can't move their eyes the way we can. So to see what's around them, owls can move their head around in strange ways.

STRANGE SCALE
MEDIUM

Whoa!

Leafcutter ants do just what their name says. They cut up pieces of leaves to use to grow their food! Leafcutter ants can carry loads that are many times their body weight. You might see them carrying huge pieces of leaves on their backs!

STRANGE SCALE

LOW

COMMON
STARLING

Birds of a feather flock together! This old saying means that one type of animal usually hangs out with the same type. This type of bird travels in huge groups. When they fly, they move in strange and beautiful patterns!

STRANGE SCALE
LOW

VIETNAMESE MOSSY FROG

These frogs are covered with yucky bumps that look like warts. Their bumps help them to blend into their mossy habitat. When they sit still, Vietnamese mossy frogs are difficult to spot!

Glossary

Adaptation

a change in structure, form, or habits to fit different conditions.

Bioluminescent

describes a living thing able to give off light.

Evolve

in a living thing, to change or develop over the course of many generations.

Fungus (plural fungi)

a living thing that usually grows on plants or on decaying matter.

Species

a group of animals or plants that have certain traits in common and can reproduce (make more animals like themselves) with each other.

Larva

the stage early in an insect's life when it looks like a worm.

Index

A
adaptations, 3
ants, leafcutter, 40-41
archerfish, 24-25

B
bears, polar, 11
beetles, click, 18
bioluminescence, 16-19,
    36-37
birds
    flamingos, 30-31
    hamerkops, 12-13
    owls, short-eared,
        38-39
    penguins, 10
    ptarmigans, 11
    starlings, common,
        42-43
    woodpeckers, 4-5

C
camouflage, 26, 37
crabs
    boxer, pompom, or
        cheerleader, 26
    coconut or robber, 27
    decorator, 26

F
fish
    archerfish, 24-25
    lanternfish, 19
    mudskippers, 6-7
    sharks, pygmy, 36-37
flamingos, 30-31

flocks, 42-43
frogs, Vietnamese
    mossy, 44-45

G
glowworms, 18
    New Zealand, 16-17
gnats, fungus, 16-17

H
hamerkops, 12-13
horses, Yakutian, 10
hyenas, spotted, 34-35

I
insects
    ants, leafcutter, 40-41
    beetles, click, 18
    See also glowworms

J
jellyfish, 18
    immortal, 20-21

L
lanternfish, 19
lizards
    basilisk, 14-15
    thorny devil, 32-33

M
macaques, Japanese.
        See monkeys, snow
mammals
    bears, polar, 17
    horses, Yakutian, 16
    hyenas, spotted,
        34-35

monkeys, snow, 8-9
    seals, hooded, 22-23
    sheep, Dall, 17
    walruses, 17
monkeys, snow, 8-9
mudskippers, 6-7

O
owls, short-eared,
    38-39

P
penguins, 10
polyps, 20-21
ptarmigans, 11

S
scuba divers, 29
sea anemones, 26
seals, hooded, 22-23
sharks, pygmy, 36-37
sheep, Dall, 11
spiders, diving bell,
    28-29
spines, for defense,
    32-33
squid, 19
starlings, common,
    42-43

T
thorny devils, 32-33

W
walruses, 11
woodpeckers, 4-5

Acknowledgments